The Grip of Darkness

by Steffon Jenkins

Table Of Contents

Preface

Throughout the course of my life, I've endured situations that literally felt like hell was here on earth, surrounding and sucking me into an inescapable abyss. I felt powerless, helpless, forgotten and completely alone. More often than not, it was incredibly hard for me to breathe. The simple process of inhaling and exhaling everyday was just too much work; I felt like I was slowly suffocating from within!

Desperation was a familiar friend, constantly reminding me of my insufficiencies. Inner struggles locked me in a psychological wrestling match with every part of my being. Each day was more of the same. Instead of dealing with my bleak reality, I focused on anything to avoid facing the dark womb of an unproductive life.

Finally, I hit rock bottom emotionally and had no choice but to deal with the fact that I lived a lie, wore a mask and lived a pretend life for an exceptionally long time.

Nevertheless God...

(John 12:24 NKJV)

Most assuredly, I say to you, unless a grain of wheat falls into the ground and dies, it remains alone; but if it dies, it produces much grain.

Over time I began to grasp the meaning of this powerful scripture. When a seed is planted in the soil and dies, it remains there alone. This death is a solitary process, which becomes the gateway to something greater than the seed ever would have been on its own. The sacrifice of one kernel of wheat ultimately produces many kernels, resulting in a plentiful harvest of new lives. Before the kernel of wheat can grow to full maturity and produce a plentiful harvest, it has to undergo a harsh yet necessary process in a dark place. Being able to embrace this truth, helped me to appreciate the importance of Christ's death on the cross. Christ died alone, was entombed alone in a dark place and was resurrected alone to bring new life to every person who would receive Him. The process of His death (by crucifixion) was lonely and agonizing to say the least; but it was also the only way for mankind to receive abundant life through the gift of salvation.

Clearly I didn't know these things years ago, nor did I understand the life process I was enduring. During those moments of so much pain and struggle, all I really had was a lot of confusion. Many of my questions about life were centered on my pain and began with the word "why".

- Why do I have to die to circumstances beyond my control?

- Why are so many hardships part of my process?

- Why have I been abandoned by so many in my life, what did I do wrong?

- Why is agony and pain connected to everything I touched?

- Why was this particular life scenario handed down to me, aren't I worthy of something better?

- Why do I have to attempt to figure out all of this alone, in such a dark place, gripped by fear and insecurity?

- Why do I constantly have to watch good things skip over my life and happen for others; very often for people who have caused me great sorrow?

- Why can't I be someone else, with a different past and a brighter future?

- Why doesn't anyone see me?

- Why won't anyone help me?

The questions ran through my mind in a non-stop swirl of self-pity, regret and sometimes even depression. Where was the moment when everything would change, or at least be made plain to me?

Wow! Looking back now, I see a broken hearted young woman, desperately trying to navigate life with so many questions and very few answers. Sadly, I wasn't a woman winning over fear, I was gripped by darkness.

Let's Take The Journey Together...

I have a question for you.

Do you remember being taught in school, that plants need sunlight in order to grow?

Well what if I told you, that information was only half true? In all actuality the most crucial part of the seeds growth cycle does not occur in the warmth of the sun's light; the initial growth transition begins deep in the cold ground, where the seed is covered and hidden in a dark place. That dark, lonely, hidden place is exactly where the seed needs to be temporarily, in order to eventually produce life and become a benefit to others.

Seeds are tiny molecule ovules, containing at their center an embryo, the "shall be"...or the *future* of the actual plant. At their initial planting, seeds lie dormant in a resting state, where they remain for a designated period of time. When the seed reaches the point where it is ready to develop, water is now required. In fact, the presence of water creates a pressurized environment for the seed, causing it to burst and begin to grow. Internally the developmental process of the seed at this stage is called germination and every seed will undergo this transition. Externally there are many different factors that govern the growth cycle of the seed. Growth processes are often unique to certain species of seeds and are always affected by both the climate and the soil the seed is grown in.

Now before the seed even hits the ground in the planting phase, the ground must be tilled, or prepared to receive it. This means all weeds, rocks, stones, and potentially obstructive debris should be removed from the planting site to support an optimal growth environment. Anything that would prevent the seed from sprouting up, should be cleared away, most especially weeds. By definition, a weed is a wild plant, which grows in an unwanted place and competes with cultivated plants. Weeds are extremely dangerous and will harm sprouting seeds or budding plantings.

They must be pulled completely out of the ground roots included, because if left unattended they will literally strangle, cause unhealthy growth to, or even kill nearby growing plants. Along with the tilling and weed removal processes, the soil nourishing the seed must be fertilized or conditioned with nutrients to produce maximum plant growth. Each of these steps are a vital component of agricultural preparation, required to ensure healthy plant growth.

Another critical element of the seeds growth cycle is photosynthesis, which is the process through which plants use light to store energy. Through photosynthesis, sunlight assists in converting carbon dioxide from the air into stored forms of energy; very much like our human bodies transform sugar into energy. If you remove light from the plant, growth continues because of the stored energy it utilizes.

Agricultural preparation, germination, fertilization and photosynthesis all work in unison to strengthen the seedling to grow, sprout up and push through the soil.

During winter months when low temperatures and darker days don't provide the most favorable growing conditions, some plants and vegetables can be persuaded to produce new crops, through the *"forcing"* process. I know you're thinking that word sounds painful, but this process can yield impressive crop results when fresh produce is scarce.

As I take you on my personal journey through the grips of many dark places in my lifetime, you will see just how much we as human beings, go through the same processes as a planted seed. Each of us is a seed, in the Lord's vineyard, awaiting our opportunity to sprout up healthy and strong; but first, we must die to self-will in those dark places of personal affliction and pain.

"The Fallen Grain"

As the child of a drug addicted mother, somehow unknowingly, I became an addict myself. I was addicted to desiring love and affection and needing to feel wanted. The concept of unconditional love escaped me and as a result, settling for tainted superficial affection in any form seemed normal. I ended up innocently looking for love, lured by the wrong faces into so many dark and despairing places.

My mother was absolutely gorgeous, with perfect hair and a flawless fashion sense. Gold earrings, necklaces and one of a kind shoe styles accompanied her unique style of dress, which was completely unlike anyone else. She didn't follow fashion trends, she created her own. She was so raw and real, with an incredible sense of humor and an abundant supply of love for her children. To me my mother was larger than life.

Sadly, there was only one thing she loved more than any of that, and that was her drug of choice. The disease of drug addiction had my mother by the throat, and she simply could not break free. No matter how much she tried, it constantly called her by name. Her desire for chasing that habit caused her to be missing in action often, in fact almost always! Oh, how I craved my mother's affection.

Don't get me wrong, I have many fond memories of fun filled times with my mom, when she came around. I can remember living with her for a short period, when I was about four years old. My bedroom walls were painted beautiful bright colors, pink stood out to me more than the rest, which would probably explain why I absolutely love all shades of pink to this day. Memories of those early years with my mother are fragmented snapshots. I remember pulling a stool up to the stove, to make my own dinner sometimes, my favorite dish was okra.

I know, I know...what four-year-old loves okra right? Another vivid childhood memory I have is of us spending time at the beach, which is probably why I enjoy being near water so much. It's feels like a place of sanctuary for me.

Shortly before I turned five, I was sent to live with my maternal grandparents. They had a huge white house, built by my grandad, who was an architect. That house was always so much fun with its creepy attic, huge basement and full garage complete with all sorts of building materials, mysterious gadgets and wood crafts. There was an expansive backyard for us to play in; and I loved the beautiful rose bushes and forsythia shrubs that grew alongside the house. My world of imagination kicked in at grandma's house; which was the ideal place to pretend I had a perfect life. Most of my best childhood memories were created while living there.

Shortly after I turned six years old, my grandad suffered a fatal heart attack on the job. I cannot say exactly how I felt at that time, but I know I missed him terribly. Things started shifting after his passing, at least from my perspective. Grandma stopped going to church, where she served as one of the ushers., and mommy stayed gone most of the time. Even though I was unaware of the full extent of what was transpiring, the atmosphere in our home felt different; it was dense with sadness.

By the time I was turning seven, my little brother came on the scene. Now it was the two of us with grandma, who had already raised her own children and should have been able to rest at this point in life. In retrospect, I realize it had to be incredibly difficult for her to take on the responsibility of raising two young children at her age, yet she did it very well. Grandma became our rock and with the help of my aunts and uncles she managed to keep up with us and the house. There was always a sense of peace at grandma's house and with her I felt content, like everything was going to be okay. That feeling was something I did not have before. Grandma had such a big heart; I can honestly say we lacked nothing in her care, except everything a biological mother's love could give. That is what I craved for most, my mother's nurturing love and attention.

Even though Grandma was a believer, I can't recall her telling me too much about God. Of course she was an example of Godly character, as far as her lifestyle reflected, but I can't say she talked to me about the Lord specifically. Maybe she felt I was too young. However, I can remember always being curious about God! The discovery of God's unfailing love was accomplished on my own through catastrophic experiences.

One of my childhood friends, lived down the street with her grandparents, they renovated a shed and used it as a church right in their backyard. I would join them for church every Sunday, singing in the youth choir, and learning about Jesus in Sunday school.

Surprisingly, they had a few dedicated members. During prayer we would kneel in front of chairs, on pillows, and call on the name of Jesus, until the heavens opened up. I had no idea what that all meant, but it sure was interesting and it captivated me. Not only was I intrigued, those experiences never left my spirit. At the age of twelve, I got saved! I was so excited about Jesus loving me enough to save me, I couldn't wait to get home and share this great news. When I arrived home, I excitedly told my grandmother what happened, that I was saved. She looked at me and asked, "...saved from what?"

Her question caught me off guard and I think she truly wanted to know if I really understood what I was proclaiming. To be perfectly honest I did not!

Desperately longing for my mother, was a craving that ran so deep in me it hurt, especially in my childhood years. Struggling with this never ending desire to be wanted by her, caused me to always feel neglected, abandoned, unwanted, and unloved. Even though I felt love from my grandma, aunts, and uncles; nothing equaled what I longed to experience with my mother. The void of her absence flowed through me deeper than a river. She was everything to me. We had a special bond but not that of your typical mother/daughter relationship. The fact that she was so frequently absent from our lives, prohibited us from developing a typical parent/child relationship.

As a result of my constant longing to be with her, I would spend hours daydreaming about my mother. One of my favorite places to be on summer days, was outside in the backyard on a blanket, gazing into the clouds. I would wonder what my mother was doing at that very moment. Where was she? Was she thinking of me? Did she want to come see me? Did she even love me? So many thoughts and unanswered questions ran through my mind that I would literally tire myself out just thinking. Then I would simply quiet my spirit and relax to the sound of the wind whispering through softly blowing leaves and drift off to sleep.

Now there were those seldom, but precious moments when mommy would actually come to the house and stay for a few days. My brother and I would get so excited, only to soon be disappointed because she would just sleep for hours. We didn't care though, having her there was more than enough for us in that present moment.

We had absolutely no idea that she had been up chasing that "high" sensation for days, and her body was overly exhausted, in desperate need of rest. We were oblivious of the dangers she faced night after night due to her lifestyle.

Then there was a time, when mommy came back to live in the house for a while. It was so much fun having her home. We would pretend to have a cooking show and make up all sorts of dishes to prepare for our imaginary audiences. She was a phenomenal dancer and we had dance shows, which she choreographed. Sometimes my friends and I would gather all of our neighbors and put on recitals right in the backyard. We had costumes and everything, our imaginations were incredible, and we enjoyed every bit of it. But soon all the fun would end abruptly and mommy would be gone again!

"It Dies Alone"

All I craved for, was to be able to experience a mother and daughter relationship, like those I saw in school with my peers. That was normal life, wasn't it? Isn't it funny how you can go through situations in your childhood and not realize how it truly effects or alters your life, until you have to take a glance back. Sometime later, my grandma unfortunately became unable to continue to care for us, so my brother and I got separated from each other and pushed off between relatives. As a teenager, I slowly evolved into my rebellious stage and stayed there for a while. You know that phase, the *"you can't tell me anything so don't you dare even try"* phase. Because I was constantly being shuffled from one home to another, I felt as if I had no concrete point of accountability. I was not in your face disrespectful to adults or authority figures, but I was on my own, so I conducted myself as if I was my own parent. I had no structure in my life, no support system, no direction, no wise advisors or counselors, and no one to answer to. I was primed and ready to be gripped by darkness!

Because I was emotionally damaged, I truly did not know exactly who to trust or believe in. Due to these increasingly unfortunate circumstances, even though I loved school and earned good grades; I began to fall off and continued falling into a dark and lonely pit. I started skipping classes with my friends, which soon turned into missing days out of school entirely. Sometimes I would just spend the day at a friend's house and other times I would just hang at the park, or anywhere I could find, in order to try and escape my reality. I was always in between places to stay, all the while struggling so hard not to literally feel the pain of what was transpiring, in this messed up thing called, my life. I was spiraling deeper into a dark place, soon becoming homeless ending up in very unstable predicaments. At first glance, I did not look like I was in lack or what people ideally think of, when the thought of a homeless person comes to mind, however I was! None of my school friends knew that I did not have a stable home, or place to stay. I was extremely embarrassed to let anyone know what was really going on. It all became a dark gripping secret, suppressed within. There were maybe two individuals at the time, who knew exactly what I was dealing with, my cousin and a close friend. There were times, I did not have any food at all, or would only have crackers and tea to eat. My close friend would sometimes cook for me, I was truly blessed to have him during that season of my life.

Who would have ever thought I would wind up being a homeless teenager, lost, afraid, lonely, hopeless and hungry at times? Surely not I.

"But God"

 There was one time I remember sleeping in a walk-in closet, at an older friend's apartment, this was my bedroom for the time being. I would get up in the morning and make a decision about attending school, based on how I felt that day.

Sometimes I would go to school just because I was starving, other times was because I wanted to be around smiling faces but most of the time, it was to hide my distress in this dark place, you know how that goes, camouflage within the crowd. This huge secret was killing me softly, it was stealing my teenage years. Those years of innocence, fun, spending time at the mall, joking laughing enjoying life. I mean do not get me wrong, I had what I called filtered fun; however, my reality was what it was. This was my life and all I knew was that, this dark place had captured me and I was dying to self! By self I mean to who I was as a human being. I was alone in so many ways and utterly confused.

At about thirteen, it was in a dark place one night that my innocence was taken without me even knowing it. How can that even happen? I know, I asked myself that same question years later when I realized that I had been a victim of rape. It was not a violent attack kind of rape, but rather a smooth manipulation, at least that's how I saw it. Can you imagine masquerading through life to the point where you convince yourself that certain things did not happen to you? I succumbed to the

"No, not me" syndrome for many years, compartmentalizing memories, attempting to tuck them away forever. During the rape, I did not quite understand what was transpiring, I just figured I had no choice but to comply, especially if I wanted to have a place to stay. I even convinced myself that this must be love until my body was replaced by another young girl the next night. She was pretty and skinny and was "loved" just like I was, by someone who was manipulating and taking advantage of us both. Now I began battling with insecurities related to my weight because I was always on the chubby side and eventually this led to bouts of depression. The drinking alcohol, smoking cigarettes, and looking for love in all the wrong dark places soon became routine practices for me. With minimal adult supervision or guidance in place, my life began to spiral out of control. Yes, I was slowly dying to self.

A couple of years later, after talking with my cousin one day, she invited me to come stay with her. By this time, I was going on sixteen and she lived in the "live" part of town, so I was all game for that!

I stayed with her for a good while and we had a ball together, but truth be told I was numb from everything that had already happened. I slowly became a train wreck, waiting for the actual collision to happen. We would go to parties, or hang out at the mall until we had enough and take the last bus home. Sometimes we hitched rides from complete strangers. At other times we would stay up all night laughing, joking and talking non-stop about everything under the sun, like normal teenagers. She was like the sister I never had. There were times when some parts of me felt completely normal, however reality was still waiting for me, when the laughter stopped, and the fun ended.

Being in this environment for the most part kept me from dealing with inner hurt, plus my cousin's mother and my mother shared life stories that were remarkably similar, so that created a unique bond between us.

She understood my situation and I understood hers.

At this time, my mom was going through revolving doors between jail and drug programs; so much so that I began to lose track of where she was. Eventually, I ended up getting a job and being able to take care of my necessities. This is where I met tall dark, and very handsome. I never really had anyone show genuine interest in me, so meeting tall dark and very handsome had me on cloud nine. Oh how quickly he became everything to me; he was funny, caring, showed me things I never experienced before, took me places, bought me gifts, fed me and was very attentive to me. I was grown now, and he was my man, the one that was going to sweep me off my feet and take me off to wonderland.

"*Yeah okay so I thought*", in my fairy tale version of romance. Silly of me to even think I knew what love was, or even what being in a relationship entailed, I was delusional and definitely dysfunctional.

After about six months or so, we all ended up working at the same fast food establishment, my cousin, myself and let us just call him my Boo. At first, all of us working together was a great deal of fun. Then it soon ended up being a huge mess of a mistake.

He became very possessive and the fun times at work soon became horrible moments of embarrassment. Yet, none of that stopped me from hanging on to my dream of being happy with Boo, so we continued dating. We moved into a one-bedroom apartment together and I thought, maybe if we live together, things will get better. I also didn't want to continue to burden my cousin, as she had extended her home to me like no one else did. I was extremely grateful to her and I'm still grateful for her kindness to this present day.

Boo and I began living together, the days became long and the nights longer. I never realized he had so many issues since I was still blinded by mine own! I thought I was living the life, but I was so delusional. Compared to being homeless, this was like heaven to me. Learning life on my own, I had no guidelines or structure, so this was my basic training into relationships "*Love Lessons 101*". Caught up in the emotion of things, I didn't take the time to study this man's behavior. Shoot, I was confused about love from the start. How could I possibly love him, when I did not understand what it was to be loved unconditionally? I was inexperienced about so many things, but through my failures I managed to learn so much.

I began to notice he enjoyed drinking and when he did his appearance changed into something even darker than I had experienced prior. He became verbally, emotionally, and physically abusive. I failed to realize that he was in as much pain as I was. Boo was suffering from his own demons; which plagued him from childhood. There were dark voids in his life and deeply rooted emotional issues, as well as insecurities he attempted to mask with intoxication. We were two misfits uniting our demons, literally causing all hell to break loose in our lives! My God what did I get myself into?

I continued to go on living a secret lie - learning, struggling, and suffering all the while. The emotional mask I wore each day covered my inner bruises, scars, pain and fears. I reverted back to that deep dark place inside of me, while smiling on the outside. I never spoke of the things that took place once we closed our apartment door. I lived in a dual reality, one outside my home and a different one inside.

I remember praying and calling on God, even though I did not fully understand how to really seek the face of the Lord. I would find ways to manipulate certain situations, such as faking breathing problems so that he would not continue beating or kicking on me.

I became a spontaneous actress, doing anything that would keep him from pounding on me. I learned to thick quick and do whatever was necessary to stop the abuse momentarily. This was so sad and unfortunate for me, but it was the only way I could close my eyes and rest during the night. It was the only way for me to gain some measure of peace.

"Forcing Happens"

One day while at work, I received a phone call that my grandma had passed away. Grandma was my heart and I could not wrap her death around my mind, I did not want to accept the truth. Immediately, I went numb and continued through the day with little to no outward response to this shocking news. Moving as if everything were fine, I was able to function carrying this sorrowful information, as if someone told me Grandma had a simple headache or something. I simply could not wrap my mind around the fact that she was gone. That disconnected from reality feeling lasted for months, almost a year actually. I was fully awake, but sleepwalking just the same.

My grandmother was my rock, the last time I saw her was when I was admitted to the hospital, after being beaten by Boo. See, he kept me isolated from my family, friends and anyone that could possibly help me. He needed that control to validate who he thought he was in my life. He believed himself to be ruler over me. He kept me far away from anyone that could possibly rescue me from his grip of darkness!

Yes, that was what I got myself into....

Prior to grandma's passing, after she had taken ill for the last time, she moved to Jersey to be with her sisters. I wanted to visit her when her health started to fail, but was unable to break away from the controlling monster I lived with. See, not only was I afraid of the consequences of making the trip, witnessing the woman who was my rock in such a helpless state was unbearable. Even when she desperately wanted to see me, I still didn't go. Sadly, I've had to live with the pain of not having gone to her when she called for me, not speaking to her, or even kissing her soft cheek one last time.

Being with a possessive and abusive individual caused me to become a loner. I didn't hang out with friends because that was unheard of and work associates were none the wiser, to the double life I lived. As a result of wanting love, wanting a good relationship, wanting my parents present and wanting a family, I became entrenched in that very unhealthy relationship. I also became pregnant.

I know you are wondering, why in the world would I go do that!

Trust me when I tell you, my mind was not in a safe or mature place. The verbal, emotional, psychological, and physical abuse I suffered daily, degraded me to a point that my self-esteem was non-existent. I didn't know my own identity and frequent thoughts of ending my life tormented me. So many different scenarios of how I could kill myself (who would miss me?), crossed my mind...but thank God, the enemy did not win!

In spite of all this insanity, I thought, maybe Boo does love me. He took care of me, kept a roof over my head, fed me and let us not forget he was a 6'4" dark, handsome and nicely built man.

Plus, he told me he was sorry after the beatings, so I accepted those admissions of guilt as love. The apology bandages were wrapped around my heart frequently and I readily believed the ole "*I am so sorry...I will never hurt you again*" lines. The apologies seemed valid, until the moment I looked into the mirror and saw a fresh black eye and winced from another round of bruised ribs!

But God had a divine purpose for my life and the seeds of change lying dormant in my heart, were ready to be watered!

Jeremiah 29:11 (NIV)

For I know the plans I have for you, declares the Lord, plans to prosper you and not to harm you, plans to give you hope and a future.

I had my son while living in a homeless shelter. It wasn't how I thought things would play out, but in spite of my mess, the Lord kept us safe. He knew the plans he had for me!

Oh my apologies, I failed to mention the abuse became unbearable when I was smacked so hard I passed out, and regained consciousness to find my white linen pillow covered with blood. I had endured enough and needed to live for my baby; so I sought out safe housing for myself and my unborn son. Pregnant and almost due I ended up in a shelter, where we lived for about six months. Living in a shelter was not my ideal plan, but it was a safe place and I was thankful. This was a season of Selah (rest) for me, a prolonged moment to rethink my future and press for new opportunities. During this time, I met a young woman who became a good friend. The shelter was depressing, but she was a light to me, in a very dark place.

When my son was almost three years old, his dad "Boo" was murdered. Now even though we were no longer together and had a horrible past, he was still my child's father and I mourned his passing. The reality of my son having to grow up without a father saddened me. Because he was so incredibly young, my son wouldn't really remember his father and this realization broke my heart. My father was alive, but absent from my life and I understood what it felt like to be fatherless. I never wanted that for my son. Boo had another child and as crazy as it may sound, I was with the other baby's momma when we received the news of his passing. She and I had become great friends and each other's support system. We made sure our children knew each other and spent time together. She took it the hardest, and it didn't help that her daughter, who was younger than my son, looked just like Boo.

As I matured and went through some more dark seasons, I experienced many disappointments and nights of depression. I became involved in relationships, but still felt an ever present void in my life. There was always that feeling of something missing. No matter how hard I thought I could love, nothing seemed to be "it" for me. Plus, I was still learning who I truly was, learning how to slowly take some of my layers off, because I was damaged in so many ways.

I started to go back to church because even in the harsh conditions of my life, there was something always pulling on the inside of me. I wanted and needed some positive seeds to begin to take root in my spirit, which was full of hurt and hatred. In my mind, I knew I had to begin to pull myself together for this little boy, my son who was now a huge part of my life. Without my own mother's guidance to direct me, without his father's provision for my son, I had to bring this baby up the best way I knew how. I had no clue what I was doing, but certain instincts kicked in, thank God. This was when I resorted back to my upbringing with grandma. Remembering some of the things she instilled in me, and the many lessons she spoke of, helped me tremendously. I had my own apartment at this point and went back to school to complete the credits for my high school diploma, while at the same time obtaining a certified nursing assistant certificate.

I had another child during this timeframe, a precious little girl and continued pushing hard to take care of my family. Finally, I felt as if I was accomplishing goals and heading in a good direction. Life presented many challenges and setbacks, but my faith was also increasing. I even began to believe with confidence, that regardless of what I went through, we were going to be alright. I started learning about the attributes of God and His powerful, undying love for creation. In the process I also began to comprehend who I really was, and how God sees me.

During this season of feeling that I was finally free from my dark and gruesome history, I met another someone. We began spending much time together, as we learned more about one another. One day after we had been together about six months, he told me he wanted me to be his wife and proposed. I was overly excited that someone wanted me to be their wife; as usual I was being a fool in love with love! At that time, I was so blinded by the desire to be loved, that I chose to ignore the red flags waving right before my eyes yet again. Infatuated with the facade of being married was my mental state.

This man seemed to have it together and was definitely eye candy, he knew it too. During our marriage, he worked extremely hard and was a good provider to myself and my two little people. Yet, there was an underlying darkness that became too obvious to ignore. He began cheating and became verbally and mentally abusive. I could not do anything without being monitored. In the marriage, I became pregnant with twins, but due to the extremely stressful environment, I lost them both. We were not even married for two years before that roller coaster ride came to a much-needed stop. That was yet another abusive relationship I did not plan for, but it had to happen, for it was inevitable in my process of dying to my way of living.

Why do I constantly repeat the same pages of life?

My life was like reading the same book over and over and over; the story always ends the exact same way.

I prepared the paperwork myself and filed for a divorce, which was quickly granted. Strangely after the divorce and some time passed, we remained friends. Our friendship was brighter than our marriage, I was even tempted to re-marry him. Yeah...NO, God will always provide a way of escape!

1 Corinthians 10:13 KJV
There hath no temptation taken you but such as is common to man; but God is faithful, who will not suffer you to be tempted above that ye are able; but will with the temptation also make a way to escape, that ye may be able to bear it.

"The Planted Seed Hungers"

While still walking around wearing my mask of many titles...hurt, loneliness, depression, oppression, abused, scared, battered; something began to happen. I remembered being ten years old, going to that little church down the street, hearing "Jesus loved me". Those lessons caused me to me weep many nights and question the conditions of my life, from a child's point of view. Why couldn't I have parents, who loved me? Why did I ever have to be homeless and struggle the way I did? Why was I left alone? Why so much pain? Why didn't I lose my mind? Why didn't I die when I slit my wrists? Why didn't I hemorrhage to death when I was beat over and over in my pregnant belly? I began to meditate on the fact that there was no way, I could have made it through any of what I experienced, if there was no God! That was the moment it all became surreal.

You cannot tell me that God is not real. Every instance of trial, suffering, rejection, pain, affliction, emotional abuse and physical abuse I endured was designed to take me out. But through it all, God protected me and always provided a way of escape for me from the enemy's grip of darkness. This made me more curious as to who this incredible man was, that had and still has so much power. Who was this man, that genuinely loves me in spite of all of my mess?

I began to develop a spiritual hunger, my heart yearned to really understand who Jesus was and who God was. I had professed salvation through Jesus Christ, but I lacked so much in the way of sound information. There was a sincere desire in my heart to understand what the dark times of my life really meant! I also began to literally *thirst* after the things of God like never before; my mindset about salvation and living for Christ was changing my life focus.

A paradigm shift took place in my life, supernatural sources of provision and doors of unimaginable favor began opening like never before. As I began to submit myself to the will of God, and fight the desire of the flesh to go my own way, my questions regarding the Lord and His sovereignty multiplied. I began to read the bible intentionally, while praying for understanding and slowly the darkness that once enveloped my life, began to disappear. The darkness of my life was being moved out and my heart was being refreshed by the illumination of the Holy Spirit.

At this time I was raising two children and it was vital that I push past my limitations for them. Things were much different now and life was no longer just about me. I worked as a certified nursing assistant in a convalescent home, as well as doing private duty cases and was doing well for myself. I learned in this season of my life that God had given me a great sense of compassion for others. Having great empathy for others allowed me to feel their pain and become more sensitive to the needs of my patients. Life was looking better and many things were starting to fall into place.

My mother finally completed a drug program successfully, was able to obtain her own apartment and started working as a drug counselor. Dancing and choreography was her passion and she was given the opportunity to teach dance for a well-established college in our area; which she absolutely loved. I was so proud of her accomplishments! We were able to start building a healthier relationship and she spent time with her grandchildren. Even though there were many lost years between us, my heart was delighted that mommy had become a part of our lives in this new and positive way. Feeling content now, but still not knowing my purpose, I continued attending church regularly, singing in the choir, and participating in bible study. My mother attended church with me a few times and I realized she needed my strength and support at this point in her life. I really felt like life had a new meaning, there was finally some light at the end of the proverbial tunnel. Or was there? Was it light I saw, or a mirage...a cruel figment of my fantastic imagination?

I became relaxed, too comfortable in knowledge that everything I craved for in life had finally been satisfied. That all came to a screeching halt one night, signaled by an unusually loud knock at my door. The sound and intensity of this knock contained a message that made my heart sink deep into the pit my stomach. I immediately felt sick, my senses were on red alert. This visitor was not bringing good news and my spirit was warning me, preparing me for a horrific announcement.

Peering out of an upstairs window, I saw two detectives standing there and everything in me froze. I couldn't think or move for an instant. Instinctively I knew what their message was. See, up until this point I had not heard from my mother in about two weeks, which was completely like her now. Since she had been recovering wonderfully, we stayed in contact daily, it was our new norm. This particular weekend would have meant she would spend extra time with us, especially since it was the birthday celebration weekend for both children. Since their birthdays are a week and a half apart, I would save money and increase the fun factor by celebrating them together.

My mother lived with her fiancé', a man she met in her recovery program. Although I respected her choice to be in this relationship, something in his eyes always frightened me and when I looked at him I clearly understood that cliché', "If looks could kill ...."

The detectives informed me they had news regarding my mother and wanted me to accompany them to the police station. They didn't have to say it, I knew my mother was gone. In my mind I saw those menacing eyes again and I knew he had killed her.

Before I left for the police station, I called my aunt who was one of the ministers at our church for prayer. I informed her of what I felt in my spirit (that mommy was gone), and told her I just needed her to pray for my strength.

When I arrived at the station the detectives confirmed what my heart had already revealed to me. That familiar numbing sensation took precedence and immediately I was gripped by darkness. Immediately, I began to freefall back to that familiar deep dark place. Her fiancé' had tortured and heinously murdered her, then simply discarded her helpless, mutilated body in the basement of the building where they lived.

What kind of person could do something like this, was the thought that took over my mind? But like I said, I was numb, so it was almost as if it did not affect me at that present time. I responded to my mother's death in the exact same manner I reacted to my grandmother's passing. I went on doing what was necessary to maintain. My personalized survival mask appeared instantaneously and I showed up for work as scheduled, as if it was just another normal day. I believed I functioned like this for maybe a month, before my supervisor insisted that I take a leave of absence.

I have waited my whole life to experience a meaningful bond with my mother, and now she was gone. Who would have known our relationship would end in such tragedy? She worked so hard to get to this place in her life, then it was snatched from her in such a brutal way.

My mother was kind, fun loving, hilarious, and full of life. In spite of all she had endured, she embraced her new lease on life with the wonder of a wide eyed child, she was finally ready to be her very best self. Mommy was so beautiful and now she was gone, without warning or even an opportunity to say good bye to those who loved her and were so proud of her life victories. The ending to her story was so unfair and I couldn't bring myself to accept it. I was so angry!

One late night as I was praying, the Lord brought my mind back a few years prior, to when mommy was on one of her *"missing in action"* ventures. I began to intercede on her behalf, not realizing then that I was in fact warring in the spirit, for God to bring her home. Her children were growing older, she now had two young grandchildren that needed her in their lives. It was time for her to get it together. Well, God did bring her home, just not the way I had expected.

Oh God, I am back here in this place, I thought I would never see this place again. Why have you brought me back here? All I heard was "There is something I need you to do" I had no clue what that could have possibly meant. Honestly, I thought I was going crazy!

When we get to a particular place in God and He is ready for us to move to another level, He will turn up the heat. The heat is not meant to kill us, but it is effective in removing undesired things off our lives; making us a suitable sacrifice for Him. This was something I did not know, until I began learning more about salvation. God required more of me and was ready for the seeds of change planted in my spirit to spring forth. It was time for them to awaken!

I was experiencing the *"forcing process"*, hurtful deaths in my life that were symbolic of the surrender taking place within me, forcing me to bow to the will of God. The devastating events I endured led me to reach for God like never before. I began to cry out to Him with a loud thunderous voice filled with despair. I needed heaven to hear me and respond. Each situation I went through caused me to learn God in a different way. Each situation taught me different lessons that were incredibly unique and totally necessary for my spiritual development. If I had not experienced those moments of transformation, chances are I would have never learned to trust the Lord, in the manner that I do now. Every bit of pain I endured was designed for my purpose and my destiny. They were uniquely created just for me, so it was good that I was afflicted.

For many years I did not respond to my mother's death and become oblivious to my own emotions. Not that I was cold hearted, but I was simply numb, I had learned to function through pain and devastations indefinitely because that was my normal. I believe it was not until about ten years later, that I finally broke down and began to pour out my grief. As I deliberately spent more time in the presence of God, He showed me myself and that I actually have a heart for His people. I went through many more fiery trials of great devastation, however, each event mentioned in this book helped to shape the very core of my spiritual foundation.

God has placed seeds of change in each and every one of us and they can only be cultivated in dark places! You must be buried in the dirt, you must go through fiery trials, much pain and varied sufferings in order for self (flesh) to die and your seeds to mature and produce fruit. We cannot explain why God would allow us to go through such anguish, difficulties, and calamities. All that is required of us to know is that going through these dark places are the prerequisite, for stepping out into the fullness of our destinies! Know that you cannot give up, it is not an option to turn back, because God made us to resilient!

"Produced In A Dark Place"

These hurtful despairing places are where spiritual muscles are developed!

Every time we are placed in unbearable situations, we get uncomfortable and begin to resist. We push back with every bit of strength we can mustard up and this opposition forces us to pray, once prayer begins yielding results, our faith is strengthened. Prayer helps us to commune, or communicate with the Father as His created beings and children. During these intimate times of fellowship God will begin to download His plan for our individual lives. He will give us peace and blessings, often releasing some of the secret desires of our hearts. Even though we don't always think so, God hears and answers our cries.

His responses may not arrive in the manner or time frame we anticipate; but we receive them never the less! His word declares that we will never be left alone or forsaken. This is our assurance that He is constantly with us, even in our dark places. Our God is consistent and keeps promises. When we cannot trace Him, we must trust that the Lord is very present!

We were made in the very image of God, His pneuma gave us life. His essence was breathed into us, therefore He lives on the inside. He is the very makeup of our DNA; this is why the spirit man will never be content until it is fed Godly nourishment. Nothing will satisfy the hunger or thirst the spirit man craves, except the things of Christ. Nothing compares to the replenishing power of spiritual nourishment!

(Psalm 119:71) states "**It was good I was afflicted, so I might learn your statues** (*your ways*)."

It's good that I die (to self-will) in this, dirt so that my seed can produce something powerful in this dark place!

So, all the while we are asking why; Jesus is asking us "*Why not? Look at all I went through for you. I suffered bled and died just so that you can have eternal life. I took on the sins of the world, so that you can be pardoned of your sins.*"

It is our nature to be afraid of the unknown and get twisted in our own emotions when difficulties arise. When we learn more about who we are in Christ and how much power we possess being a chosen generation with Kingdom citizenship, the obstacles don't seem so difficult.

We do not have to run and hide or wear masks to hide our pain. We don't have to be ashamed about the issues of our past or feel defeated; for the word of God states that we are more than conquerors through Him that loves us. Jesus loved us so much that He gave up His life in order for us to live. How awesome is our God!

In Him we are made new creatures, all that old hurt, that old pain, and every devastation we encountered is passed away. Just knowing that alone, should give us inner joy as well as strength to continue to press through whatever is before us. The word tells us that the joy of the Lord is our strength, I thought I was surely headed for death many times over, but God had a sure plan for me that included the strength to choose life over death. Guess what? His plan was mandated before I was even conceived. As I was going through some of the darkest periods of my life, the plan of God for my life was being cultivated. Those gifts and callings that he placed within, were being watered and matured in dark places, to bud and come forth in due season.

Wow, that is amazing!

Listen this is vital for you to know.

In our deep dark places, the enemy will have us believe that we are useless with no purpose or power. The enemy's main career goal is to destroy humankind "prematurely." It is his job to suffocate us, strip us of everything before (*pre*) we come into the realization (*maturity*) of what is planted on the inside of us. We have the Greater One dwelling within us, who reigns over the devil in the world. This is why it is imperative to build a truly authentic relationship with the sustainer of our lives. Jesus Christ is the one who gives life, the one who planted those seeds of hope, change and deliverance within our hearts.

There is greatness lying dormant waiting to germinate inside of you. The word of God fertilizes the seed and the Holy Spirit is the refreshing water that creates a pressurized environment in our lives, which cracks the seed and brings forth new life.

It was not until I got tired of my pain and became hungry for a change that I decided to chase after Jesus.

In my ignorance I was initially running *from* my life, not towards, but in the opposite direction of the only one who gives life. I had heard enough about Him, tried everything else, even tasted a bit of the Lord's goodness. However, I hadn't fully submitted to the process of change the Father was trying to present to me. I needed to be filled by something that does not fade away, something that would keep me no matter what I faced, something that would give me a strong and unshakable foundation.

Please don't get me wrong and don't misunderstand what I'm saying; storms will still rise up in our lives, but we know that God can quiet any storm. Without the presence of spiritual challenges our faith cannot be tested, growth will not be increased, and we will not learn how to trust God wholeheartedly.

Remember I mentioned the process of forcing earlier in the book? Well this was that process.

Everything I had endured up to this point "*forced*" me to hear God's call. Those bottomless pit seasons, forced me to come to Him, call on the name of Jesus and sow tears of repentance at His feet. Those moments forced me to recognize there was something greater on the inside of me. Those moments forced me to see God's grace, which caused me to truly look in the mirror and begin taking off the masks I lived behind for so long. There was no longer any need to hide all of my pain, when I could simply lay it all at the altar.

Every bit of what I endured forced me to increase in strength, to keep pushing forward in life and begin sprouting. The word of God states in **Matthew 17:20**, that all we need is **faith the size of a mustard seed.**

Well did you ever take the time to really find out what that scripture means?

A mustard seed is no larger than the tip of a pencil, but when placed in dark dry places it can grow into a large shrub about six to twenty feet tall. The dark dry place creates the perfect breeding ground for the mustard seed to germinate. The germination process does not affect every single mustard seed in the exact same way. Every seed is unique, just like you and I. We are all human beings, but no two people are exactly the same. Isn't that just like God? We're all going through a germination process, however, we are all uniquely made, so we're not handling our processes in the exact same manner. So what forces you to sprout up, may not work for me. What causes your seed to awaken may not do the same for me.

When we are placed in fiery trials, going through dry wilderness seasons, and caught up in dark lonely periods, they are only designed to cause us to germinate, to grow into our purpose.

Most importantly remember there must be a connection to the source (*the Son*), because authentic relationship is imperative. Having light enter your dark place is vital and Jesus is most certainly the light of the world! Even though we are processed within a dark place of trial and suffering, it is the light of God that pierces that darkness, in order to give us energy (*Holy Ghost power...dunamis power*) to walk in our destined purpose!

If we were not exposed to these conditions, we would never come into the knowledge of our "*Shall Be*". You "shall be" is who you were created to be in the Kingdom of God. It's the thing the enemy has worked so hard your entire life to keep you from discovering!

Please know exposure to these conditions will not overtake you, they will not kill you, they will however, kill those things that are not pleasing to God that reside within you.

You must understand both who you are and whose you are! Who you are and whose you are may sound the same, but in fact they are distinctively different. Who are you in Christ? Why were you created? What is your position in the Kingdom? These are powerful questions that most definitely require a Selah moment of reflection for serious consideration.

You must clearly understand *whose* you are, know the God you serve and embrace the benefits He has designed for you and your life. By reading the bible, get to know how God feels about you...understand what He expects of you...realize the great sacrifice Jesus Christ extended by laying down His life for you.

There are so many questions to be asked and answered about God and His relationship with humanity and we won't receive the answer to every question immediately; but know this, as responsible believers we are encouraged to seek to know Him as much as possible. As Kingdom citizens, we have a charge to search for this knowledge.

It does not profit us anything to call ourselves Kingdom citizens, yet have no idea as to who we are, what purpose we have, and what our rights or citizen benefits are!

The answers to these questions will begin to transform our minds and lives and we grow and grace and knowledge. Gaining this information allows us to conduct our lives as God intended us to.

Once we decide to follow Christ we are new creatures, old things are passed away as we press forward into the newness of God. We cannot live our lives based on who other people say we are, or even what we may have once believed about ourselves. So many of us are guilty of that, as I know I was for an awfully long time. I did not know who I was, and for many years I was trying to measure up to someone else's standards. I was so confused I lost myself in someone else's identity. The only one we should lose our lives for is the Lord, as we surrender ourselves to him daily.

"The Birthing Process"

As believers we become unstoppable when we seek after and receive the wisdom of God.

When the enemy comes in like a flood, the word says that God will lift up a standard against him. The Lord will cover you, so that you will not be affected by the flood. You will not be drowned; it will surely pass over.

Once our seeds are ready to sprout, a birthing process begins. Just as it is in the complex process of natural childbirth, there will be hard labor pains, prolonged pushing, and an intensive time of travailing. All that is needed is for us to breathe in the process, bear down in the Holy Ghost, remain in a fixed position in Christ through His word and push through opposition when it is necessary. Imagine if you will, all of your purpose laying inside the embryo of a seed. Through life's adversities you have survived much hardship with the seed still in place, still intact. It has received the proper nutrients, saturated with living water, and now you anxiously await the moment of awakening. Suddenly, you realize there really is greatness inside of you; but there is still uncertainty as to what will spring forth at the appointed time.

The enemy and his camp desires our seeds of greatness and they will go to great lengths just to have them. This is why we are in a constant warfare, not only with the enemy of our souls, but within our own flesh as well. The enemy desires to have our visions, our purpose, our destiny and our promises, but thanks be to God, the promises of the Lord are always yes and amen. We have the victory through our Lord Jesus Christ! The steps of a righteous man are ordered by the Lord and what God has predestined for us will not fail to manifest in our due season.

Do not give up, do not allow the enemy to take your seeds prematurely. What God has for you is for you. You will have to face some deep dark places in order to discover who you are, but allow your spirit to be okay with knowing God is always with us.

By no means is this a process that happens overnight, it is actually a day by day journey that we have embarked on. It takes time for purpose to establish roots in our lives and grow. It takes time for us to mature into our purpose. Allow God to force you (not with anger, but with unconditional love) into your

"*shall be*" experiences. His way is mighty sweet, trust Him in your good times and in those times you are faced with unexpected challenges. He is God all by Himself and does not change; however we must seek after Him with earnest sincerity and dedication. We must let His word till the ground of our hearts, which will clear away emotional debris and psychological clutter so that He can perform a spiritual pruning process. This work of the Holy Spirit cuts away the dead overgrown stems, weeds and bushes of our past that threaten to hinder or choke out the growth of budding miracles in our present lives!

Psalm 51:10

Create in me a clean heart Oh God, and create new a right spirit within me.

There were points in my life that I thought I was going to die for sure. When I reflect over those moments from a spiritual vantage point, I realize that death did come to certain things I once allowed to overtake me. Fear, doubt, depression, self-hurt, pain, self-sabotage and a dysfunctional mindset all died in my growth process. I had to face each of these areas of my life in order for my individual purpose to even become tangible. My growth process is not the same as yours and yours differs from the next person; we each have our own walk and journey. We don't always know, but the Lord is always clear about the way we must take.

Even when we make mistakes, the Lord knows what the end results of those moments will produce. They were no surprise to him and guess what? He can take care of them too!

Jeremiah 1:5 NLT

I knew you before I formed you in your mother's womb. Before you were born, I set you apart and appointed you as my prophet to the nations.

God knew each of us and established specific plans for our lives even before we were in our mother's wombs.

Yes, He knew my mother would struggle with drug addiction issues and how that would affect her destiny. He knew how short our time together would be after I became an adult and we rekindled our relationship. He knew she would fight unbelievably hard to get clean and sober and would then be murdered. He knew my heart would break many times, but that I was resilient and would develop new strength in the process. There is quite a bit more that I could share about my life, but if I did not have faith in Christ, I can honestly say I would have not made it through any of what I've written about so far. God is real and desires to have a real relationship with each of us. I encourage you to accept Jesus Christ as Lord and Savior...ask Him to come into your life and take full control. Invite Him into the dark places of your struggles and allow the light of God's truth to show you the way out. This is truly the best decision you will ever make.

Being a believer does not make you exempt from life's problems. Being a believer gives you peace in knowing that the grace of God provides strength during your weakest moments. He is a covering and a shelter over your life that is constant and cannot fail. The Lord will take care of you in ways man has no power to.

He will truly provide a way of escape from the distressing situations you encounter in life.

I should have lost my mind over the years and trust me it almost happened; but God kept speaking to me and telling me I could make it, I wasn't going crazy, I was someone special and I had something important to do for Him. So, I kept praying and believing the promises of God while continuously pushing forward. He sent individuals to cross my path at different seasons in my life, and they helped me get closer to where I needed to be in Him. God knows who we will earnestly listen to and He will send just the right individual to speak life into our situation. Their voices will refresh our spirits and cause seeds of hope to spring to life within us!

Being a seed of Christ is just like being the negative to a photograph; in order to bring forth a beautiful picture that negative must first be placed in a dark place. Embrace the purpose connected to your dark place and know that when you come out, you'll bring something beautiful and life transforming with you.

Know this, your voice, your story, your testimony, your journey and your life experience is assigned to a particular audience.

What I learned in my suffering will surely save others from a life of hopelessness. Even if it would be just one life then sharing my story is not in vain. I am fully persuaded, beyond the shadow of a doubt that there is hope in God. He has definitely given me life and that more abundantly! Do I have everything I imagined I would have obtained at this point in my life? No, not yet, and there is no complaint in my heart concerning the matter. I will continue to wait upon the Lord until my change comes.

The grip of darkness that repeatedly attempted to sabotage my life, actually contributed to causing the divine greatness within me to manifest. There is so much more to be birthed, as I continue my journey.

My process is far from over, as a matter of fact, in many ways it is just beginning! I have to believe and hold fast to what I have learned throughout the years. God is not a man who lies, in fact He *cannot* lie; so His promises will surely come to pass.

The word of God is the blueprint provided for our lives that teaches us what to do's, how to do's, and what not to do's of this journey. Once we focus on and learn how to apply these instructions to our lives, we will begin to sprout up and push through every dark experience with determination and confidence.

God offers healing for the pain of yesterday, hope for today and a promise for our future. We tend to run to God when we experience difficulties beyond our control and we should do that. However, when we learn to run to Him in our everyday living, He literally becomes our guide, illuminating our path and showing us the way to go.

Many of us have dealt with sad and unfortunate experiences in life, from being abandoned by people who should have loved us, to being assaulted or abused by people who should have loved and protected us. Some of us are products of broken homes, addicted parents, extreme verbal abuse, psychological isolation and generational strongholds, which have crippled us in unimaginable ways. Those things will never define who we are, so we will continue to seek the Lord's face for total healing and deliverance, knowing that God is a deliverer of them that seek Him! He can fill any void and heal any hurt. His love for us is sufficient for every one of our needs and we can rest assured that there is no age limit, or cut off time for you to start a relationship with the Lord. If you have faith just the size of a mustard seed than all things are possible with God.

Precious reader, I pray that you will be encouraged to keep pressing and moving forward; do not give up and never give in. The seeds of promise planted in your spirit will most certainly break through the grip of darkness you have endured.... and push you to reach for the light!

Psalm 27:1 NASB

The Lord is my light and my salvation; whom shall I fear? The

Lord is the defense of my life; whom shall I dread?

DEDICATION:

To my children, Jamul Swope ll, De'najha Willis, and Ricky Dawson lll, it has always been my desire for each of you to be proud of me and know that I love you unconditionally. Much of my inspiration to continue fighting and pressing forward, was because of you. Thank you for all you have shown me about myself, especially when it comes to motherhood. As a young mother, there was a great deal that I simply did not know, and I realize I didn't get everything correct. However, I have learned so much on this motherhood journey with you and I'm still learning every day. Yes, we have our struggles, but God is yet faithful and I am so blessed to have you. Each of you has added greatness to my life and I am so proud of the young men and women you are and will continue to become. I love you guys so much and I want you to know it is never too late to pursue your dreams and passions.

Ricky Dawson, you are one of my closest friends. First, I want to thank you for being such an awesome dad to our son and to our other two grown people. Since the day we met, you have been a consistent tower of strength for me. You are gentle, kind, funny, and peaceable. In so many ways, you were the breath of fresh air, that I so needed. You have shown me what unconditional love is and exemplified the true meaning of a faithful friend. Your encouragement reassured me many times over the years that I would make it through certain situations and of course, you were always right. Thank you for genuinely caring for me and pushing me to become my best self. To this very day, you remain a trusted and loyal friend; I would not change you for the world. I am forever grateful to God for allowing us to have our moment in time (many years), and I pray God's blessings over your life. I love you always.

I would also like to thank my business coach, Evangelist Beverley Vaughn for extending her wisdom and guidance to me. Your relentless pursuit of business intelligence, as well as your total commitment to each of your coaching clients is absolutely unbelievable. Thank you for showing me how to embrace my unique process and shift my mindset to evolve as a multi-dimensional entrepreneur. Thank you for pushing me beyond my norm, because you knew I could handle it and for all the great opportunities you've presented to me. Most of all, thank you for believing in me! I will never forget our first meeting; we sat down, began talking and very soon after tears began flowing down my face. You gave me some hard "truths of the matter" which caused me to dig deep. This is the result of my digging. Coach, I DID IT...The Grip of Fear No Longer Has A Hold on Me!

Last but definitely not least....To the woman of God that locked jaws on me like a pit pull, and would not release me, until I produced! I would like to give a huge heartfelt and sincere thanks to my mentor,

Prophet Erika Erkard. Because of you, I have such a strong desire and craving for the word of God. I've learned so much from you, throughout the years. Thank you for not giving up on me and for continuously pushing me in the spirit. You challenge me to always be prepared to see "what comes next". You saw both spiritual and natural gifts within me, before I even knew they existed and you've never allowed me to settle for less than I can accomplish. I can honestly say that none of this would be a reality, if the Lord had not orchestrated our divine connection. Thank you for all the prayers and intercession on my behalf and for literally going to bat in my defense in certain areas. It is a pleasure and honor to have been mentored by you.

I bless God for you in ways I cannot fully express. I love you and appreciate all that you have done, not only for me but for my family as well. You are the best, please know that your labor has not been in vain. **#IAMFRUIT**

The Author: Steffon Jenkins